A Void and Cloudless Sky

poems by

Ricki Cummings

Finishing Line Press
Georgetown, Kentucky

A Void and Cloudless Sky

Copyright © 2021 by Ricki Cummings
ISBN 978-1-64662-560-4 First Edition
All rights reserved under International and Pan-American Copyright Conventions. No part of this book may be reproduced in any manner whatsoever without written permission from the publisher, except in the case of brief quotations embodied in critical articles and reviews.

ACKNOWLEDGMENTS

"Another Poem Titled 'Your Grandpa Was Like That: Listened a Lot and Didn't Talk Much'" and "Maybe He Will Make Enough Money to Subscribe to Earth" originally appeared at *calibanonline*

"Weirdness Magnet" contains a line from the song "Bring Me Your Loves" by St. Vincent, and a line from Kurt Vonnegut's "God Bless You, Mr. Rosewater"

Thanks are in order to all my friends, enemies, colleagues, and peers without whom this book would literally not exist. Thanks in particular to Meredith Yayanos, Tony Trigilio, Elizabeth Olson, Shannon Elward, and Harley Anastasia Chapman for their kind words, contributions, and assistance in bringing it to life.

Publisher: Leah Huete de Maines
Editor: Christen Kincaid
Cover Art and Design: Elizabeth Olson, http://zoem.me
Author Photo: Ricki Cummings

Order online: www.finishinglinepress.com
also available on amazon.com

Author inquiries and mail orders:
Finishing Line Press
PO Box 1626
Georgetown, Kentucky 40324
USA

Table of Contents

Concatenation 1

Another Poem Titled "Your Grandpa Was Like That: Listened a

    Lot and Didn't Talk Much" 4

Coming Out in Idaho 9

Exiting 13

Ralph's, Moorhead, MN 14

Tom Waits 15

Maybe He Will Make Enough Money to Subscribe to Earth 17

Symphorophilia 19

Arctor 20

A Poem Wherein Everything Goes as Expected 21

Weirdness Magnet 23

Growing Up in Public 25

Concatenation

eight bytes of yellow dots
on a page to track ideas
this is all honest thievery
and of three dreams
of car crashes & kaiju
the music is to disengage
the cerebral cortex
a lizard brain patois shortcut
narrative is arboreal
bits of time wound
around chair legs
and infrared remote controls

the cat ate the last puzzle
piece you found it by your
ankle pinned and screwed
in place the man offers
knowledge in exchange for a job
nailed to a tree and sacrificed
to himself ravens piercing
sides it's hard to tell in the heat
skin dry and glands dry
and lungs dry and the rain
torn like a sheet
it rattles when it all
comes together or
it sizzles like cherry steel
quenched

when it startles

is when it's working
no elephants in these parts
there are no gay people
in Chechnya I don't think

we have anything like that
in our country
plans for the day
backlogged entries empty
agendas forgotten
erased it seems cryptic
but there's always
the word coalesce

the solar system was once
a disc of dust the moon
was once the earth
now fragmented tiny
blacking the whole
of the spiral center
captured umbral
the corpse will be auctioned
at the address below
if word is not received
notice is given: decision
covered in ash and blow

a fragment of syntax
and a man surviving
a plane crash by sleeping
becomes necessary
a flaming chariot
pulled by dragons
transporting the dead
words & words and music
by patti & bruce
and screamed for decades
things but in ideas drinking
pisswater to own the libs
institutions to change your life

they go in through your nose
and let you keep the little
piece of brain they cut out smiling

the originals were all frauds

novels
the dreaming said once
accrete

Another Poem Titled "Your Grandpa Was Like That: Listened a Lot and Didn't Talk Much"

I speak to The Common Man
when I say "Remember the Krebs Cycle,"
for indeed we all must stop
and breathe
from time to time.
This was going to be
a quick Dickinson ballad,
maybe a haiku,
but Death kindly stopped for tea.
Someone recently told me
on Twitter
that one of my favorite comedians
was an asshole
as if I wasn't already aware,
but he also put the greatest pigeon
pun of all time into a joke
about the Kennedy assassination,
so who's the real asshole here?
I spent the better part of a month
learning how to build
a robot that writes poetry
based on the works of HP Lovecraft
and now I'm not so sure
what's real and what's the bot.
It picks out n-grams—
strings of words—
and then reassembles them
according to esoteric math
using modules with names like
TensorFlow, which really isn't
that far off from namedropping
Cthulhu or the Black Goat of the Woods.
Here's a kitchen sink,
for good measure.

(For future generations: the answer
to the question
of what is this poem about
is the body.
Always the body.)
"I don't see why they have
to shove it in our face,"
says my mother to my face
when we talk about my
attraction to men
and my predilection toward
hobbies socially engineered
to keep me poor and possibly dead.
In the abstract, I do not exist
in this booth, across from her,
eating eggs I am allergic to.
We somehow managed to read
the same book and come
to wildly different conclusions.
Sometimes I think I understand
the tendency for black metal bands
to murder each other
and burn down churches,
but other times I think they do it
out of boredom.
So anyway, the Krebs Cycle.
The mitochondria is
the end of this sentence.
When ATP is split, a tiny
amount of energy is released,
which then gets redirected
into reconstructing ATP.
The human body is a perpetual
nowhere machine continuously hanging
in bootstrapping.

Adenosine triphosphate, by the way.
That was going to burn away
at the back of your mind
all day, I'm sure.
Nearly twenty percent
of the blood sugar in your body
is used by your brain
to process this stupid shit.
Aren't you glad you're here?
You could be arguing with your mother,
or actively harming your intestines,
or fucking a stranger, or sleeping,
and yet this reconstituted tree aspic
causing the air to vibrate
is what you've chosen.
There was supposed to be a metaphor here
but instead it's maps and pins
and bits of string and wild hair
and cigarettes and unemployment.
I remember
that one of the purposes
of poetic alliteration
is to pull the reader
or listener shrieking
through the work,
so maybe they forget for a little while
how what is said
doesn't quite make sense,
told slant, as it were,
and full of allusion that doesn't
quite fit. Six
years and I still don't
think it's right.
What I mean is this:
in an automobile drivetrain

we must take into account
the fact that the wheel
on the inside of a turn
is actually moving slower
than the wheel on the outside.
This is simple geometry, yet
it breaks bones.
I noticed last night
there are people I'll never see again.
For the first time,
it hurt. Sometimes I don't
fall asleep until the sun comes back up.
I don't know why. Sometimes
I repeat myself and I do know why.
Sometimes I tell myself
that bitches get shit done,
but it never seems to work for me.
I end up on a beach
with knifed-up crabs who speak
what sounds like Spanish
but might be Italian—something
Latin, regardless. The crabs,
arthropodan and sideways,
seem concerned with my keyboarding skill.
I tell them bitches get shit done,
but they seem to want none of that.
Imagine yourself running on a beach,
pursued by crabs unconcerned
with your productivity,
but obsessed with your
ability to communicate. You should
have stayed in school. Went
for more than two years
of a foreign language.

Lived in central Europe. Stayed
in your genetic lane. Now
it's all eye stalks
and crustaceans. You're fucked, bud.
Down to eating peanut butter straight from the jar.
But what do the crabs signify?
We don't even know what
kind of crabs they are. Hermit crabs?
Alaska king? Whichever ones are the sideways
walking ones, most likely. That
probably narrows it down to something like
a hundred species. Can someone
Google that? Kidding. Don't bother. Unimportant.
What is important is that we recognize
that crabs and humans
require oxygen to run their animal asses
across the beach
and to sit steaming in a diner.
Cellular respiration, it turns out,
is so complex that the interaction
of proteins and transport networks and broken
bonds can only be described by a diagram.
So I draw my mother a picture.
Here is a normal person, say, you. Here
is me, also a normal person. And my
mother, she insists:
"You'll always be my son."

Coming Out in Idaho

I woke up
to my brain
skipping frames
like an old movie
or a video card
pushed beyond
its limits
when attempting
to render
a world.
To look for joy
do not look
for meaning.
A beep.
To look
for a girl
do not her
vulpine rictus,
teeth ablaze.
We see
conspiracies
everywhere
in order to
make order.
Do not over-
celebrate
this newfound
knowledge;
who yet knows
what lurks
in the universe's
deepest holes?
Popping bass
and discs on fire.

Filter sweeps.
When I was young
I'd drive
until almost lost,
then circle back
to the turbine,
its low blade groan
and midnight
power thrust
into the sky.
Gravel
and ethylene glycol.
We'd drink til
the dogs came into
the bar, then
offer the dogs
drinks. Ralph's
no longer exists,
replaced by
a granite sign
and sod.
Fragments
and stoplights.
Radiohead.
Driving
stone sober
on deserted
sidewalks. Stopping
for directions.
That's where
we had our first
kiss, in the rain,
a living cliché.
Do not look.

Only ghosts
now and then.
I was walking
down the stairs
for breakfast,
skipping class.
Syncopation
and French
twelve-tone mass.
Collisions
and near-misses.
Knowledge
comes at a cost:
sex or death.
Curiosity is
insatiable
like sex or death.
Spiraling, the same
fletchless arrow.
My heels come
from the men's section.
Masculine and blunt.
Two pairs of cardinals,
three chickadees,
one of them
albino,
and a bluejay.
Sent as harbingers.
Assassins. Symbols.
Every day
is a plan
for dying.

We are a fever
dream. A migraine
of the heart. Or
shared blood,
an explosive thud
against the pelvis,
triggered by stress
and cured flesh. A
flicker at the edge
of the ventricle.
The left
to the body.
A straight line
must become
an arc
because nature
isn't perfect
like that.
I sleep in
rotations now,
like the weather.
Vortices of dreams
and memory.
If only
putting words down
was as easy
as picking them up,
as easy
as sleep, as rain.

Exiting

The snake lopes across the desert,
eyes clouded, blue within blue, skin
dull and cracking, searching
indistinct for a rock or some edge
to break upon, to tear the space
between scales and slither through,
rebirth after birth, shining new
and sleek after being found again and again.
The snake, of the sand and in the sand
and among the sand, does not know
why it sheds its skin, except that the skin
is uncomfortable, that it cannot contain
the snake, who knows only air and sand.
Behind it, the snake leaves a part of itself,
a ghost ominous and clear. The snake,
refreshed, breathes deep, its many
hundred ribs expanding. The breeze
rolls the shed skin across the sand from the rock,
skipping through the snake's triplet track.

Ralph's, Moorhead, MN

I think I'm in
a situation
again, drunk
and chatting
about a stranger's
dog she brought
into the bar.
Can you even
bring a dog
into a bar?
It's spring,
and cold still,
snow on the ground
and a snapping
wind—it would be
cruel to leave
him out there.
My drinking
partner, on his
fifth round
of pints
for a quarter,
loves this dog,
a beautiful
black lab,
and all I can do
is stare
at the cracked
vinyl booth
to keep
from being foolish
in front of a dog.

Tom Waits

That's twice now I've come
across the name
Kurt Weill
and the rain and thunder
fails to arrive.
They make films about
the Butterfly Effect,
but nobody mentions
the assertion that, according
to noted users
of hallucinogens, the DC
Comics universe is an
organism that controls
its own actions.
Theater happens everywhere,
but it's usually delivered
by way of caterwaul
or doll-faced witches
in black leather.
The intertextual hypersexual
neural network
devours Derrida and shits out
Bill Hicks. Even the best
comedians know when good
puns are necessary. The punch
is dictated by time
and consequence
long ignored.
Threepenny pulp is what
we all grow up on, whether
it's paper or trombones or the telly
or cels or beamed into
the goddamned *brain*.

And every side
every side
will tell you that it's wrong
to like ballet and box wine
at the same time,
but everyone, at some point
in their lives, has been
Tom Waits eating flies
in *Dracula*.

Maybe He Will Make Enough Money to Subscribe to Earth

i don't really necessarily believe in synchronicity except when it's clearly the universe trying to tell me something. if i dream a dream and then it comes to pass, what does that mean. a short repartee about the disembodied head of jack kirby with one of the few professional magicians i know (by which i mean actual magic, not street magic), classroom discussion of Breton, and now this: there's something buzzing around in my head.

have we, in fact, given birth to hyperreality. maybe, as philip k. dick said, we have participated unknowingly in the creation of a spurious reality, and then we have obligingly fed it to ourselves.

something about the absolute faith in the power of metaphor, in words as conjuring, of television as sigil, of hypertext as hypertime. all history is linked through the written word, the present is a continuous persistent hallucination transmitted instantaneously from my head to your head to the heads of your friends.

apparently there's a hidden little alcove where you can walk down and watch a 5-10 minute snippet from james burke's *connections*. not being versed in bbc science specials, i had no idea who this weirdo spouting things about a future network of knowledge was, but i latched onto a particularly salient line and backtracked.

given that consensus reality seems to be breaking down by the moment, we can think ourselves into a better universe. if phil can accidentally write the book of acts and then also relive his own story eight years later, who is the author of that reality: god, the author of luke-acts, philip k. dick, or the chaotic vibrations of slowed energy.

incomprehensible, maybe, but not stupid.

one in which he is talking about the concept of 'supers' in television—the superimposed text over a moving video background—and how they mostly don't work in comics.

it's no coincidence that my favorite works all collapse time and distort memory, an effect of influence, a conglomeration of disparate threads converging.

am I seeing connections that aren't there.

is omni-time even necessarily better.

is there an algorithm there that I'm not seeing.

i don't know.

Symphorophilia

it's been a long time coming. a suture wriggling to the surface. this advent birth. bridging anticipatory. it churns. waiting to molt biological slurry. brundlefly. tetsuo cyberpunk body horror wrapped in a neat midwinter rebirth.
parenthetical metastasis—store-bought is fine—revulsion cracked mirrors and singularities absorb all reflect nothing but slant. where is the body? scuttling. roiling in undertow. drowning under neural floodwaters. it is metastasizing memetically along a carrier wave of bytes and copper electrons. the body carnal and digital. biomechanical lust. a male-to-male coupling under red laser light.
touchscreens. haptic delay. squelch and static. lips and feedback drone. extra bones in the foot. a ringing of the eyes. metallic vomit, reflective of all time, shuddering with breath.

Arctor

Handlers, always, constructing
and assisting, eyes through the mouth
or throat swallowing static.
Points in spacetime connected
by fiber optics and vaporwave.
Mickey Mouse, inside the suit
it's me and it's me or it's me.
I think these high-rises are
fictional constructs built on
the shared belief in rebar
and dopamine pathways.
The left hand does not know
what the right brain is thinking.
Ambiguously dexterous. I once replaced
a concrete rock in a park
with a real rock: the video is hilarious:
here's a whole crew of Imagineers
dumbfounded by the real within
the unreal, a stone unturned,
a single side up and just as effective.
Few words seem as suited to their task
as "scramble," no matter the context.
Eggs. Jets. A foot race to blue flowers.
Dyes and sleight of hand.
The fucked-up black swan part
I couldn't remember. Not
that I was trying. I remembered
involuntarily wrong.

A Poem Wherein Everything Goes as Expected

One night I got lost
in my own house.
All the rooms were
the same, but different.
I walked up and down
the halls and stairs,
looking for a book, I think,
and then myself.
I'd fallen through the floor.
Not as if a crack had
appeared like a gaping
fault in a movie,
more like I slid
through it, like a sheet
of ice, down into a room
I know did not exist.
Could not exist.
I'd already checked
where this room should be.
And yet, here I was,
in a room I'd never seen
but definitely had become
a part of my house when
I wasn't looking.
I have been concerned
about the difference
between why and how,
and how why is oblique
and why how is concrete.
How I got there was easy,
I fell frictionless through
the floor. Why
I got there, though,
seems less oblivious.

This room that doesn't
exist in the space I'd
already been, a dusty double
of cinderblock
and a single mousetrap
with ancient cheese
and cobwebs holding
it down. I remembered,
then, a dream of a spider
crawling onto my hand
and biting the flesh
between my thumb and forefinger,
on the pressure point
that leads to the cervical
vertebrae, and then another
dream wherein a small
snake bites the same
spot, casually, filling
its mouth with my blood
all the way to the back fangs,
where childhood legend says
garter snake venom is released.
I am calm and observe the snake,
who is not angry or hungry,
only sending a message
to my brain stem.

Weirdness Magnet

I say *Bring me your finest collection
of weirdos* and the waiter nods and returns
with a blue heeler and four small rocks.
I hug each tightly, then line the rocks on the sill
and let the dog herd butterflies and grasshoppers,
like Ferdinand smelling flowers
under a cork tree.

> *Bring me your loves*, she sings, and I
> shiver in torn pleather. My breath cracks
> icewater. This is new ritual, and the single caught
> sob
> nearly runs me into a brid[g]e piling.
> I like to tell people I am a witch
> because if I say it
> it makes it so. I have to tell them
> I'm joking
> when I say my retirement plan
> is waiting for a nuclear exchange.
> They don't laugh as much as I do.

Pink slime is a beef slurry used to concentrate
calories, lower fat content, and alarm the general public.
It runs under the streets and leads to outbursts
of emotional distress. I have a general theory about
food additives. The waiter doesn't care;
he's too busy handling the table of lobster claws.
They seem to want the Wellington, but there's
an obvious language barrier and everyone is having
a hell of a time. So much for articulating.

I traced a sign for protection on your back and it seemed
to only half work. I'm not sure what I did wrong.

Maybe we were still too close to it.
Shelley says that all poetry comes from an excess
of passion, and at 29, all passion is excessive. Expulsive.
When one is upon his second marriage
excess seems the only answer. There's some
design flaw here. *What to do* I ask the waiter
between snapping claws *when the cause and the cure is the same?*
And the librarian, quietly pulling a seat up to the table,
says *You've got to be kind.*

Growing Up in Public
for Lou Reed

I could never answer
a fireman
a policeman
a spaceman
any kind of man, really.

The world rusts
like an old county
bridge. I want to kiss
so deeply that I can flick
the inside of your sternum
with my tongue, and make love
like it will save me
from drowning in a lake
of leaves and train tracks.
I want to feel the electric hum,
the galvanic touch
of sweat and blood and sex
that vibrates down to anti-muons.

Mostly I lie in bed and wait
for nothing in particular
to come to mind, and it comes.
I sit in the dark in the bathroom on the cold vinyl tile
made to look like stone.
I wait for visions, or voices, but none come.
I empty myself like all the Jacks suggest
and *still* the passing thoughts are about
my lack of passing thoughts.

After masturbating, Ginsberg heard
the voice of William Blake.
All I ever hear is the voice of my racing pulse
and the whining whistle of low-grade tinnitus.
I knew Jack Spicer, sir, and you are no Jack Spicer,

married and with child and poorly dedicated
to love and linguistics. Your favorite
organ is the clitoris.

Ask me now what I'd like to be
when I grow up. An Irishman. A woman.
A tall, smoldering brunette in stockings
held in place by garter snakes and seams
running from struck heel to crushed head.
I want to be a drunk full of Berkeley
and a headful of acid rain, pitted breasts
and hollowed eyes. A white picket fence
between two dazzling blondes in Dior A-lines.
The curve of Audrey Hepburn's jaw. Boot leather.

Catalogue, ideologue, cartographer, dictionary;
a tool to stir the stew and mouldy genetic
necklace of oyster boils and aqua vitae and matters
of country. I'd like to be a head of state
of emergency. A quick bawdy pun and the corps
becomes non-corporeal, the press secretary laughs
like shrieking steel, the walls fade into the
Parkway, and the stars in the asphalt become
the eyes of America, overrun by cars
and the light pollution of a thousand-thousand
neon signs proclaiming victory over sex.

I want to be the song of crickets: ever-present,
unsettling, beautiful.

Ricki Cummings was born in Grand Forks, ND, in 1981. Since then they have lived in North Dakota, Minnesota, Indiana, and Illinois, with extended periods in Idaho.

Upon the third stint as an undergraduate, Ricki discovered that poetry was one of the few things they were good at and also enjoyed, eventually adding an MFA in Poetry from Columbia College Chicago to a bachelor's in General Studies, an associate's in Interior Design, and a minor in Creative Writing. This eclecticism—or indecision, if you like—has led to poetry with influences from the personal to the pop culture, from Walter Benjamin to Walt Disney, from Deleuze and Guattari to Simon and Kirby, from Lorca to Cronenberg.

Their poetry ranges through themes of home, self, reality, family, gender, love, death, sex, and structure. Their interests include sci-fi videogames, cats, and industrial metal that uses audio samples from Kubrick films. They once remarked "You know, for being a poet, I don't actually read poetry a lot," despite having several linear feet of shelf space devoted to it.

Currently, Ricki lives in Chicago with their spouse, child, two cats, and seven guitars. One day they plan to have a queer commune where they can spend the day reading, writing, and sleeping. Until then, they spend the day reading, writing, sleeping, and doing the regular domestic labor of running a home.

They've been called a good housewife.

www.ingramcontent.com/pod-product-compliance
Lightning Source LLC
LaVergne TN
LVHW041518070426
835507LV00012B/1667